```
YOUR NAME HERE
GUIDE TO LIFE
```

Author: Michael Rosenbaum
Designer: Danielle Howes
Copy Editor: Barbara Rose
Product Development: Melissa Giovagnoli

This publication is intended to provoke thought and share opinions about life and life lessons. It is based on the best insights and judgment of the author, but does not offer professional advice or counsel of any type or recommendations regarding any specific individuals or their situations.

© 2009 Barosum Books
All Rights Reserved.

For more information or to send comments, please e-mail: info@barosum.com.

ISBN 978-0-9825016-2-7
LCCN 2009905528

For Dad,

a great listener, teacher and storyteller, whom I miss every day.

It's About Time, Don't You Think?

Aren't you getting just a little bit tired of reading books about other people?

Especially *those* people?

You know the books I mean. There's the one by the 14-pound model describing her secrets to beauty:

1. *Be born with perfect genes.*
2. *Have a daily massage with sea salts from the Sargasso Sea.*
3. *Hire your personal chef from the Anorexia School of Culinary Science.*
4. *Did I mention the perfect genes?*

Or maybe you're fed up with celebrity guides to happiness:

1. *I was giving and giving and giving to my fans, but I wasn't doing nearly enough for me, me, me.*
2. *After my fifth divorce, I finally discovered the secret to love, and I am still joyously happy after three whole months with Alejandro.*
3. *And the children simply adore our nanny, who is almost as much a mother to them as I am.*

Or CEO memoirs:

1. *All my employees agree I'm the best boss they've ever had.*
2. *I hated to fire dad, especially since he started the company, but leaders must make the tough choices.*
3. *And so many people doubted me when I graduated 30th in my class at Harvard.*

What's wrong with all these books, other than the smug, self-satisfied, revisionist histories on every page? Glad you asked. The truth is that there's little we can learn from the rich and powerful, the incredibly successful and the genetically blessed.

Their stories are like ours only tangentially. Their lives and, worse, their terribly flawed memories, offer only thin insights to the rest of us.

If you need proof, simply ask your personal trainer, your nanny or your executive chef.

What this world really needs is a book inspired by the stories of real, normal, down-to-earth people. People with kids and crises and bills and failings; cops and psychologists, entrepreneurs and dishwashers, cab drivers and office managers. People with jobs and mortgages and families and maybe a few extra pounds they'd like to get rid of…

People like you. And me.

Everyday people are the best teachers, because their lives are like ours. They always end up in the slowest line at the bank, just as we do, and they get the same runaround we experience from tech support. We know them, because we are the same people.

Even better, the people who inhabit our offices, schools and neighborhoods are ready to teach us something new every day. All we have to do is pay attention. After enough time, the insights can fill a book.

Like this one. Written especially for a not-quite-famous, but terrific friend.

Written for *you*.

So send your personal chef home for the night, hand the kids over to the nanny, cancel your personal trainer, and relish a few stories about the lives we share.

Enjoy.

Thank You

I'm not sure it takes a village to raise a child, but it requires a small town full of friends, editors and kibitzers to create a book. As we grappled with the tone of the text, titles, topics and typefaces over the past year, I've been blessed with dozens of people willing to offer their insights on any and all subjects.

I'm most grateful for the guidance provided by Melissa Giovagnoli as we developed the concept, the title and, ultimately, the theme for the *Your Name Here Guides* series. Thanks to Dani Howes for a nifty cover design and to Barbara Rose for a professional editing and cleanup of the text.

Thanks as well to all the people who read the book, voted on cover designs, commented on title options and kept me on pace to stop talking about it and get it done already. Nearly a hundred people took part in bringing this project to completion, and some of them are actually willing to be recognized for their roles.

My gratitude goes to Diane Aboulafia-D'Jaen, Dave Armon, Janet Bergman, Bruce Bloom, Darcy Bretz, David Brimm, Alan Caplan, Donni Case, Ed Diamond, Steven E. Eisenberg, Esq, Seth Eisner, Chuck Field, Tony Fiorentino, Gerald F. Fitzgerald Jr., Pat Fitzgerald, William G. Gardner, Naomi Gitlin, Sunny Gold, George N. Goldman, Shelley Stern Grach, Dwight E. Grimestad, Doris Haims, Jennifer L. Harris, Bill Hass, Aimee Holleb, David Inlander, Kirk James, Carol Jouzaitis, Dan Kadolph,

Antje Kalov, Betsy Katz, Julie A. Katz, Michael Kaufman, Dani Kehoe, Howard Lifshitz, N. Carol Lipis, Jeffrey London, Jeff Lukas, David Mandell, Joan Mazzonelli, Carol Metzker, Jerry Meyerhoff, Marlee Millman, Pat Moroney, Allan Newman, Tim Padgett, Bryan Paull, Gregory Paull, Linda Rosenbaum Paull, Nancy Pratt, Shep Pryor, Michael Regan, Allan Reich, Christina Renshaw, Richard Rice, Barbara Rose, Carl Rosenbaum, Jill Rosenbaum, Larry Rosenbaum, Stephanie Rosenbaum, Susan Rosenbaum, Sheri Terebelo Schiff, Jonathan Schwartz, Marilyn Seymann, Rich Shuman, Emily D. Soloff, Gabrielle S. Stormo, John Thomason, Barry R. Wallach, Paul E. Weinstein, Todd Bernard Weinstein, Mike Wien, Marcee Williams, Craig Wilson, Tom Witom, Lea Sigiel-Wolinetz and probably a dozen others whose names I have failed to include.

If you like this book, it's because the people listed above made it better.

MR

Share Your Stories

What life lessons do you want to share with us? What insights did we miss in this book and what stories should be included in our next volume?

Tell us how you learned an important lesson about life, friendship, parenting, business, or anything else you think the rest of us should know. If we include your story in a future volume of the *Your Name Here* series, we'll give you full credit as the contributor and pay you $100.

The process couldn't be easier. Simply visit our website at www.yournamehereguide.com, click on the "My Stories" link, and send us the life lesson you think we all should know.

We know you have important insights to share and we can't wait to hear from you.

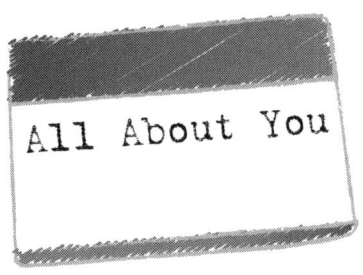

All About You

As our title suggests, this book is all about you.

Yes.

You.

I know what you're thinking. *"What about all the other people reading this book? Won't they think it's about them?"* Of course they will, but, just between us, it's really about you.

And why not? Don't you deserve to have a book that focuses specifically on you, your needs and your challenges? Isn't it about time somebody paid attention to the kind of issues that are uniquely yours?

Yes, yes and yes.

Of course, it's easy to write a book specifically about you because I know you so well. For instance…

As I recall, you got decent grades in school, but you could have done better if you didn't blow so much time on people who really didn't matter in the long run. You didn't get to be valedictorian, but at least you didn't have to take freshman biology three times, either.

You've received some recognition along the way, but it's not like you were elected president of the chess club *and* crowned at the prom. You still keep in touch with some people from school, but there aren't that many who are really, truly your friends.

You're an adult, according to your driver's license, but you don't always feel like one—and nothing at all like your parents. They were old when they were ten. On the other hand, every so often, you hear yourself saying things your parents said to you and...

Okay, how much do I really know about you? Am I at least as accurate as your high school counselor? Sure, I am. And I'm not even stalking you or stealing your text messages. Nope, I know you because you're normal. You're proud of some things, embarrassed by others, not completely sure where you're headed and at a loss to explain how certain people—you know who I mean—are doing so much better.

My Story...

- _____
- _____
- _____
- _____

It's the human condition.

In a world of six billion people, 5,999,999,999 of us aren't the smartest, richest, funniest, dumbest, goofiest, poorest or any other kind of "-*est*." Sometimes, you think you're all alone, that nobody could appreciate what you have to deal with. *(How could they? Nobody's pain is like my pain!)* At the same time, you're everyman. You're normal, the one with common sense who personifies the mainstream. Your opinions are shared by all smart people, decent people, people with both brains and hearts.

And there you have the essence of you. And me. And almost everyone. Sometimes, you think you're all alone and nobody can understand you. At other times, you think you're the prototype for normal. And sometimes, in a brilliant contradiction only the human brain can create, you believe both those things at the same time.

So there you have it. This book is all about you.

Because you're unique.
Just like everybody else.

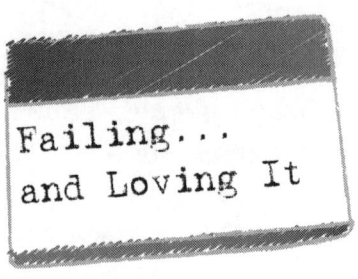

Failing... and Loving It

You gotta love failure. Love it to bits. Caress it like your best friend. Accept it as a lifelong companion. Why? That's where you'll spend most of your life. Not just you, of course. Everybody. Sure, there are some things we do without thinking, like breathing or getting a handful of popcorn to our mouths. Mostly, though, we spend our lives not making the team, not winning the lottery, not getting the lead role, not getting the corner office, not, not, not.

We're not alone. Big-league baseball players get to be heroes by reducing their failure rate to only 70 percent. Ray Kroc was a blender salesman without much of a future when he met the McDonald brothers. Bill Gates dropped out of college.

An old colleague used to say, *"The only reason we're at this company is that we failed at our last jobs."* He was right. Even though we didn't get fired from our prior jobs, we didn't stay because we weren't advancing as far or as fast as we thought we could. We failed to achieve what we hoped for at those companies, so we moved on, tried again and, maybe, did a little better. After a while, we got to be more and more successful.

Every so often, you run into someone who seems to have God on speed dial, winning or coming out on top all the time. It could happen, of course. With six billion people in the world, somebody has to get lucky almost all the time. Ask the seemingly lucky ones, though, and most will tell you about all kinds of traumas along the way. Dig deeper and you find that some of the most successful people still cannot get past some earlier failure. Some even think of themselves as failures, despite their ultimate success. What a waste.

All of us fail. That doesn't make us failures. Move on.

My Story...
- _____
- _____
- _____
- _____

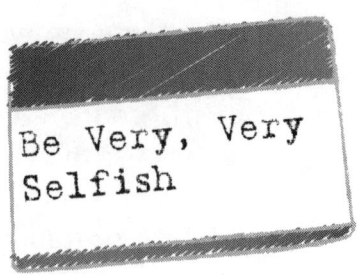

Be Very, Very Selfish

Like I said, this book is all about you. Only you get to learn from it. Don't even try to use this book to help anyone else. It won't work. There's only one person we can change and that's ourselves. When it comes to life lessons, it's all about *me, me, me*—or, in your case, *you, you, you*.

We can be nice to people, help old ladies across the street, bring over some tapioca pudding after their homes burn down, all that stuff. We can set a good example that leads someone to say, *"Golly, I'm going to work really hard so I can be more like you!"* But we can't change them.

Heck, we can barely muster the energy and will power to change ourselves. If you think you can read this book and solve someone else's problems, this would be a good time to take a nap. If you're sleeping, at least, you won't do any damage.

"But wait," you say. *"Isn't that what this book is about? Are you not trying to change me?"*

No, my friend, I am not. First, like the late Mr. Rogers, I like you just the way you are. Second, I give serious cred to the ancient Chinese adage (Why aren't there any *new* Chinese adages?) that a person who saves another's life is responsible for the person who has been saved. Frankly, my insurance company and I couldn't handle the responsibility.

More than that, I'm a realist. I've learned, usually the hard way, that we can't change other people. Books, advisors, doctors and friends work at the periphery, affecting our lives only as much as we allow. We can change people's circumstances and we can offer insights or role models they can choose to incorporate into their lives. Or not.

You can read this book, and others, and decide to adopt some of the thoughts and attitudes you encounter here. Or you can ignore them, one and all. Only you can determine which choice to make.

My Story...
- _____
- _____
- _____
- _____

Real change is about *us*, not *them*. It's about how we respond, feel and think. As well as anyone knows us, nobody is smart enough or patient enough to get into our heads and guide us through the process of change. But *we* are smart enough, if we take the time and make the effort.

Like embezzlement, change is an inside job.

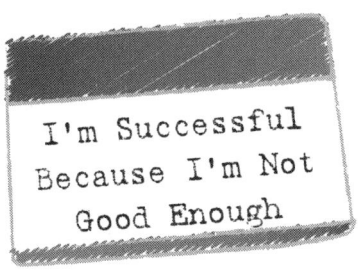

I'm Successful Because I'm Not Good Enough

I know a guy who hated to see his mom struggling with overdue bills and collection agencies. He vowed that he would never be in that position when he grew up. So he worked like crazy and let nothing stop him, and he became financially well off. I know another guy who never felt he was loved—or particularly lovable. He became a salesman and began to associate each sale with the acceptance he felt he couldn't get elsewhere. Over time, he became financially well off.

And, after becoming financially well off, neither one of these guys could relax. The holes in their souls were just too big. No amount of money, no degree of approval, no level of sales was enough to make them feel secure. One could argue, objectively, that they had achieved their goal. Subjectively, however, they could never be truly successful.

When you talk to successful people about what truly drives them, you often find they are struggling continually to overcome some sense of loss, of diminishment, of failure. Some of the most financially successful people in the world are trying to fill a void by achieving in business what's missing from their psyches. It's not about an objective degree of need or failure or trauma. It's the relative importance to them that makes the difference. The more driven the person, the bigger the hole they're trying to fill. Or rather, the bigger the perceived hole.

This might not be the case 100% of the time. But if I were a betting man, I'd like the odds.

There's nothing wrong with this, by the way. Being driven by the need to prove something is normal and it's a great source of ultimate achievement. When you're driven, you find a way to get somewhere, and that's good.

The challenge, though, is to know when to stop. If we never earn enough, if we never run fast enough, if we never turn the heads of all the strangers we meet, we can never feel secure. And if that's the case, we guarantee that we will see ourselves as failures forever.

All of us have some gaps to fill, some obstacles to overcome. When we achieve our goals, however, we have to recognize that achievement. Otherwise, what was the point of all that striving in the first place?

When you've won the race, stop running.

My Story...
- _____
- _____

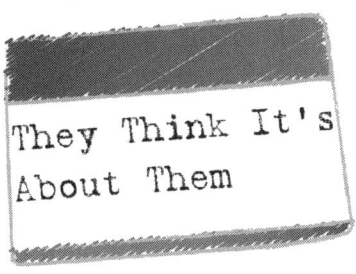
They Think It's About Them

I was always a better manager than leader when I was running a business. I knew where we needed to go; I allocated resources efficiently and developed productive programs for clients. Within the company, however, I was far less successful at inspiring loyalty and buy-in from the people who were assigned to implement the plans.

It took a while to figure out the problem, but eventually I learned my lesson. While I was focusing on the company and our clients, I didn't truly understand the motivation of employees. I took it as a given that they would see things the way I did—after all, I was *everyman*.

But things didn't work out that way. Each person in the company had individual drivers, fears and insights. When I failed to recognize and connect with these, I failed to motivate the people.

This is the most profound aspect of human relations and, like many truths, it is so simple as to be confounding. When it comes to personal growth, it's all internal. When the topic is influence, it's all about the audience.

No matter how important the speaker, no matter how

inspirational the speech, every presentation is filtered by every individual in the audience according to one standard: *"What's in it for me?"* And there's nothing wrong with this. Every speech, discussion, memo or e-mail is a transaction in which the speaker seeks influence and the audience seeks value. Value can be defined in any number of ways—education, inspiration, entertainment, profit—but it's always the value perceived by the audience, not the speaker.

Truly great leaders aren't defined by their vision, their strategy or, unfortunately, their decency. Leadership is the ability to inspire someone else to become a follower. And a person who decides to follow invariably sees an opportunity for personal benefit.

In everything we do, we need to be leaders. We don't have to be leaders like Gandhi or Moses or Churchill, but we must inspire somebody to follow.

Because it doesn't matter whom we are dealing with; it's our goal to influence their behavior.

My Story...
- _____
- _____
- _____
- _____

You'll have to convince the plumber to show up before the whole house is under water and you'll have to convince your boss to give you a raise. You'll have to cajole the maitre d' to give you a table that's actually outside the men's room, and you'll want to convince your friends not to go to the bar where you got drunk and embarrassed yourself and broke up with your ex.

Sometimes, all you need to do is ask. After all, people generally want to feel good about themselves, and being nice can make them feel like saints. You know the feeling, because you get it, too. When you do something nice for somebody else, you're doing yourself a favor, as well.

So this book is all about *you*, because *you* are *my* audience. When *you* face the world, however, it's all about *them*, because *they* are *your* audience. No matter what you want to achieve in this world, you almost always have to convince someone else to participate in the process. When you make it about the audience, you make yourself more successful.

Great leaders and natural salespeople, along with many psychopaths, make this connection instinctively, but all of us can learn how to apply it to our own lives.

Make it about them, even though you know it's really about you.

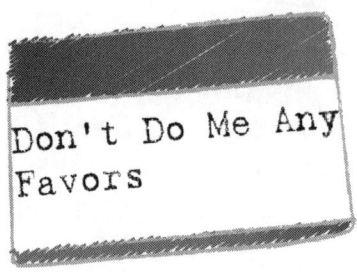

Don't Do Me Any Favors

After he came home from World War II, my dad went to volunteer at one of the veterans hospitals. When he met with the volunteer coordinator—or whatever they were called back then—the woman wasn't exactly grateful for his help.

"Don't think you're doing these men a favor by coming here," she told him. *"And don't think you're doing this for them. You're doing this for yourself, because you feel guilty that you came back in one piece and they didn't."*

And dad didn't get offended by the tirade because the woman was right. He did feel guilty about coming home in one piece and he was doing it for him. Even though he was offering to help other vets, he knew he was looking to help himself at the same time.

That's not a bad thing, of course. Most of the time, when we're doing good deeds, we fulfill a need to feel better about ourselves. It makes us better people, more praiseworthy, more in tune with God.

We get into trouble, though, when we insist we're doing it for somebody else. That's when we look for gratitude, for payback, for credit and adoration. And the adoration is never quite enough, is it?

I had a friend in college who had the right attitude. She'd type up papers for the fingerly-challenged among her friends and I told her one day that she was proving to be a real savior to a lot of people. She responded that she liked doing it, because helping others made her feel better about herself.

Praise is nice. Appreciation is welcome. It feels good to be known as a person who helps friends, feeds a family, gives to charity. But it's also important to recognize our own self interest in this. We're fulfilling our own needs and that's okay.

> *Any time we do a favor, at least two people benefit.*

My Story...
- _____
- _____
- _____
- _____

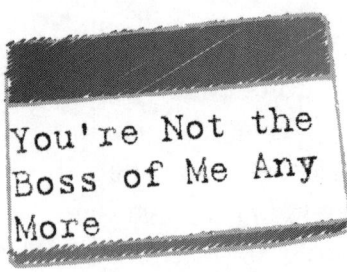

You're Not the Boss of Me Any More

As Wall Street and the economy collapsed in the fall of 2008, it was impossible to find anyone who had actually made a mistake along the way. Every captain of industry who appeared before Congress or the media—the same bold leaders who earned tens of millions by being the people who made things happen—suddenly claimed victim status. No excuse was too convoluted and no hoop too fiery for these business leaders to jump through, as if avoiding blame was an Olympic event.

All of us on the receiving ends of their alia culpas found them to be weak, unconvincing, disingenuous and, unfortunately, still much richer than we will ever be.

We mocked them, as we should, but many of us failed to recognize that we often fall into the same pattern as our suddenly naïve Wall Streeters. When things go wrong, we blame somebody else.

Maybe you blame your dad, your high school counselor, or the significant other who dated your best friend (Whom you still think of as your best friend? Really?) behind your back. Maybe it's your boss, the cabdriver who couldn't find the banquet hall in time for the wedding or the coach who didn't give you enough playing time.

I once held a grudge against a grade-school friend who used trickery to win a position I wanted. I thought about it, brooded about how my life would have been different if he hadn't cheated me.

And one day, in one of my more lucid moments, the truth slapped me. If this guy had the power to change the direction of my life, then I needed him to make things better.

What kind of deal is that? I don't talk to this guy anymore. I don't even know where he lives or if he's still alive. But I spent more than a healthy amount of time assessing the damage he had done to my life. And if I contacted him, what could he do about it? Maybe he'd promise to make it all better. Maybe he'd just laugh at what an idiot I was for holding a grudge so long.

And he'd be right. Many of us end up in this trap, blaming someone else for a gap in our lives and putting our self-esteem on hold, waiting for an apology or a cure from someone who probably doesn't even remember the situation and who doesn't matter anyway.

My Story...

- _____
- _____
- _____
- _____

Why don't they matter? Because they don't have any power that we don't give them. Like Dorothy, we're wearing the ruby slippers. Ultimately, it's our power to make the changes we need to make. People have power to hurt us because we give them that power.

Sure, some relationships are more complicated or intricate than others. We make trades and deals with bosses, spouses, children and friends. But the underlying truth remains. A boss can yell, a friend can betray, but it's our power to decide what comes next.

Do we view ourselves as victims, depending on someone else to make us whole? Do we decide we could succeed if only *they* would let us? Or do we take the responsibility and move on?

We make ourselves weak when we give others power over our lives. We get stronger when we take that power for ourselves, even if it means taking the blame more often than is comfortable.

Only the powerful can handle accountability and only accountable people become truly powerful.

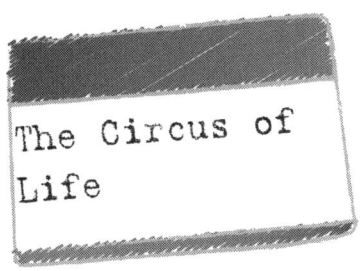

The Circus of Life

I love the circus, with all the noise and excess and the wide-eyed joy on the faces of all the little kids in the audience—including me. And I always looked forward to the annual tour of *Ringling Bros*. and the late Gunther Gebel-Williams.

Gebel-Williams worked with elephants, tigers, horses, pretty much any kind of big animal. He was the guy who did the famous American Express commercial (*"Do You Know Me?"*) with a leopard resting on his shoulders.

Gebel-Williams always seemed to get more out of the big cats than other trainers. His act was truly a ballet between one man and a dozen beasts. After he retired, nobody else quite filled the bill.

Then, one year, the regular lion tamer was ill, or had an illness in the family, or something, and he wasn't going to perform in Chicago. And Gunther Gebel-Williams was going to come out of retirement to fill in during the emergency. For a supposedly grown-up person, I was way more excited than I should have been, but who wouldn't want one more chance to see the legend?

I bought my tickets and sat through the show and the incredible Gunther Gebel-Williams came out and, let's be frank here, the act was awful. No energy. No excitement. It was like he was sleepwalking through the performance, and so were the cats.

It was confusing at first, but then it all became clear. Gebel-Williams didn't train these animals. He didn't set up the program. He was, in fact, doing someone else's act. And, most likely, he wasn't doing it as well as the guy who put the act together in the first place.

Doing someone else's act didn't work for him and it doesn't work for us, either. We always seem a bit unnatural, a little bit false, and never quite at our peak when we try to mimic somebody else. Whether we're asking lions to jump on top of an elephant or speaking to a group of co-workers, we're always more effective when we're in our own skin.

Nobody applauds when we do somebody else's act.

My Story...
- _____
- _____
- _____
- _____

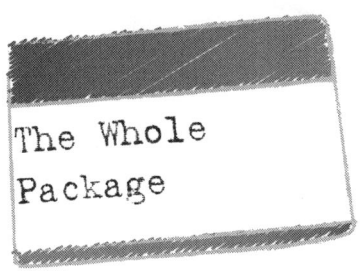

The Whole Package

"She's my best friend, but I hate her," my daughter said. She meant it, too. I don't remember the situation that led to this outburst. I don't even remember which daughter it was. But the statement stuck with me because it defines perfectly the trap we set for ourselves all too often.

It's not really possible to hate your best friend. You can hate something they do, of course, but you can't hate a person and like them at the same time. If you hate enough things about them, they stop being your friend. And if you want to stay friends, you have to get past the things you hate.

I have friends who are cheap, fake, racist, sexist, dumb, self-centered and unreliable. (Don't tell them I said this, or everyone will ask me who's who.) I don't like these people *because* of the traits listed above. I like them *in spite of* those shortcomings. If any one of them was cheap, fake, racist, sexist, dumb, self-centered and unreliable—all at once—that would be too much to deal with and we wouldn't be friends.

You know people with questionable traits as well, and sometimes you feel uncomfortable with their shortcomings. You think you should say something, for their own good, of course, but then you decide to let it go. You feel a bit like a coward or a hypocrite, but you decide not to put your relationship at risk.

Often, that's a good decision, and for two important reasons. First, they probably think you're cheap, fake, racist, sexist, dumb, self-centered or unreliable and they're holding back the urge to tell you your shortcomings—for your own good, of course.

Second, and more important, this is life. You don't get to manufacture a friend who meets every one of your criteria. You have to take people as they come—and they come with flaws. Just like jobs and software and diamonds and everything else in the real world.

I like my job, but I hate my boss. I want the applause, but I hate the rehearsal time. I like the ocean, but I hate when my hair gets frizzy. I want all the good things that I like and I don't want to deal with anything I don't like. Waaaahh. If there's something you want, something you like, be prepared to deal with the bad along with the good.

The bad stuff is just the price of admission.

My Story...
- _____
  _____
- _____
  _____

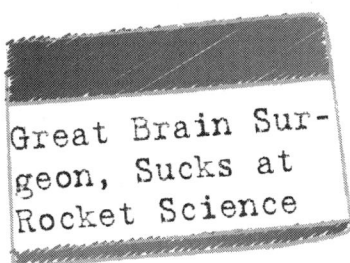

Great Brain Surgeon, Sucks at Rocket Science

Years ago, when I was covering the federal courts as a newspaper reporter, I was amazed at how frequently doctors were victimized by financial scams. Doctors tend to be smarter, work harder and become more successful than the rest of us. Medical smarts don't always translate to financial smarts, however, and busy doctors who think they're smart can become fat targets for someone with a winning personality and a plausible business concept.

Even if we don't have M.D. after our names, we're a lot like them.

We're all good at something, not so good at something else. Everybody's talent base encompasses a hundred different traits (singing, analysis, memory, looks, etc.) and each trait rests somewhere on a spectrum.

Me? I'm pretty good at crossword puzzles, not so hot at carrying a tune. I'm great at spotting patterns that make things comparable, but truly rotten at recognizing people I've met only once or twice. I know how lots of things work, but I can't repair them. In short, I'm normal.

Most of us have talents that fall somewhere near the middle of the line between great and awful. Almost all of us can identify something that we do better or with less difficulty than other things. It's our greatest strength. It's what we rely on to get things done.

Our greatest strength is a gift, but it's also a trap. When we're really good in one area, we focus on that strength and pay less attention to other parts of our lives. Practice hard enough to win a gold medal in skating and you probably won't become a football star. Spend all your time painting and you're not likely to become a great race car driver.

No big deal, most of the time. So what if I can't tune an engine? If I sell enough paintings, I can hire a mechanic. Most of us get along just fine by relying on our strengths for success and paying less attention to the things we kinda suck at. But we all have blind spots, areas of vulnerability created by the fact that we focus on our strengths without remaining aware of threats coming up from behind.

My Story...

- _____
- _____
- _____
- _____

Talent that's off the charts—or near it—is always, always, always matched by a gap somewhere else. Even a skill set that's only halfway down one end of the spectrum creates a large gap in the opposite direction. Most of the time, ignoring these gaps is no big deal. Still, it's a good idea to check our blind spots every so often.

Our greatest strength is also our greatest weakness.

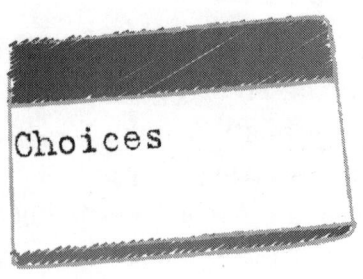

Choices

Quick, what's the most overused and misused word in the English language? Nope, it's not *paradigm* or *empowerment* or even *Brangelina*. The word in question is *can't*.

People say, *"I can't"* all the time, but almost invariably they mean, *"I won't."*

Can't is a great excuse, but it's almost always a lie and everyone who hears it knows it's a lie. Sometimes the only person who doesn't get the point is the person who *can't*. The listener might be too polite or intimidated to say, *"You could if it was important to you,"* but that's absolutely what they think. Most of the time, they're right.

It's all very liberating, of course. If I can't stick to a diet and I can't go back for my master's degree and I can't get away from the office to attend my daughter's recital, then I am free to do anything and everything else—and no one can hold me accountable.

After all, I *can't*. I'm a victim, powerless against the cruel vultures of fate and cosmic irony. Sure, I'd love to get to the wedding on time and I really should go to that funeral. And I really should lose some weight, because

I'm so fat I can't even fit into my socks any more, but I just can't.

Your best friends won't say it, so they've asked me to say it for them:

Bull.

You're making a choice. Do or don't. Go or stay. Buy or save. Diet or burst. Do whatever you choose to do, but just don't tell me you *can't*.

Some things are easier than others and any one of us can point to some physical limitation that keeps us from slam dunking or singing in the opera. If you're thinking of pointing out that you really, really can't play in the Super Bowl, forget it. That's not what this is about and you know it.

What we are talking about are the hundreds or thousands of times each year when we tell people—worst of all, ourselves—that we can't do something that,

```
My Story...
  •  _____
  •  _____
  •  _____
  •  _____
```

really, we could do if we wanted. If it's really important to us, we choose to make the effort. When it's not that important, we don't. And we reveal quite a bit about ourselves and our values when we make the choice to say we *can't*.

"I could put $25 in my 401(k) this week, but I choose to buy five triple frappalattes instead. I could help my friends move into their new condo, but I choose to watch the ball game. I could go find a better job, but I choose to sit around and complain about this one, instead."

We're always making choices, even when we pretend to be victims of some cosmic warden. Some of our choices work out well and some don't. But when we forget that they *are* choices, we make ourselves victims, and victims are weak. You can do this if you want, but why would you make that choice?

> The power of choice is the power to choose.

Avoiding Insight

Nobody learns anything while talking. When we talk, we're teaching or complaining or boring people to death. But we aren't learning. They learn about us, but we simply run our mouths.

The only way to learn is to listen, to watch, to absorb what's going on. When you're talking, someone else is learning. They might be learning things you don't want to reveal, but that's your problem.

Listening, by the way, means *listening*. Not patting people on the shoulder and saying you understand and making sure you nod or say, *"very interesting,"* every few minutes so you look engaged. Whoever came up with the concept of *"active listening"* was an idiot. Any time you're thinking about gesturing and responding so you can help the other person feel validated, you're not listening. You're acting and, frankly, you're not all that convincing.

Likewise, listening is absolutely not the same thing as waiting for your turn to talk. You know what I mean. I've seen you sitting on the edge of your seat, fidgeting while you wait for a break in the conversation so you can talk about how the exact same thing happened to your cousin's best friend's uncle's third wife. You're waiting, in reality, for a chance to make the conversation about you.

Stop it.

> There's no limit to the wisdom we can obtain if we shut up and pay attention.

My Story...
- _____
- _____
- _____
- _____

No-Returns Policy

Have you ever had someone tell you, *"Be honest, I want to know what you really think?"* And have you ever made the mistake of telling them what you really think? Have you repeated this mistake, or was once enough?

I have the searing memory of hurting someone very, very close to me. I won't go into the details—I hope this person has forgotten the trauma—but I answered a question honestly and saw the color drain, the eyes mist up and the lip quiver as the pain of my "honest answer" became overwhelming. I think about that moment every time someone asks me for my really, truly, don't-be-afraid-to-be-blunt opinion.

Every so often, people want the unvarnished truth. When that happens, it will usually be a person you know very, very well and it will be an important private conversation between two adults. Otherwise, what the other person almost always wants is validation.

When somebody asks what you really think, or you find yourself needing to tell someone an important insight—for their own good, of course—you have two immediate choices:

1. Say it.
2. Don't.

Unless someone is about to walk into an open manhole, number two is the better choice 90 percent of the time. Yes, there are times when we really must address an issue that's causing real damage, and we'll discuss those times later in this book. Most of the time, however, we're talking about a personal preference or prejudice and it's almost always better to wait.

When my daughters were in show choir, the choral director would admonish them to *"save it for the bus,"* to keep their comments to themselves until the group was together with no outsiders and nobody to be hurt by overhearing personal judgments.

My Story...

- _____
- _____
- _____
- _____

Good advice, even if there is no bus. Often, our personal judgments and helpful comments are misinterpreted by the people who need our sage advice the most. They think we're being critical or mean or flippant. They know we cannot possibly understand their pain, their challenges, how other people have hurt them before.

And once we offer our view, it's out there. Forever. We can't chase the words across the room and drag them back to be unsaid again.

You can't unsay it.

The Most Powerful Person in the Room

Want to be the most powerful, influential, admired person in the room? Want to be invited back?

Bestow blessings.

This is so obvious that we forget it again and again. Yes, it always seems like the whiners, complainers and nitpickers get their way more often than they deserve and, probably, they do. Sometimes, giving in is the path of least resistance and polite people seem to have *"Welcome"* stamped across their foreheads. Ultimately, though, folks end up avoiding negative people and gravitating toward the positive ones.

It's simple, really. People like people who like them. Tell them they're doing a good job, admire their taste in decorating, praise their fashion sense and, voila, they'll see you as far more insightful and intelligent than before.

People won't just think of you as insightful. They'll begin to think of you as the arbiter of what's good and bad, right and wrong. They won't see you as a demigod or supreme maven. But people will respond to you differently.

And why not? The person who bestows blessings is making a judgment and, therefore, comfortable enough to voice an opinion. The person who tells others they are okay, that they've made a good decision, that they are liked or trusted, makes those people more comfortable and secure. Weak people are always looking for affirmation from others, or for someone to blame. Strong people provide that affirmation to others.

There are limits to this blessings business, of course. Your blessing has to be believable, for one thing. You can't like everything about everybody, and you're just going to look weird and stalker-ish if you suddenly build a shrine to them. Compliment people on things that they know are flawed and they'll recognize you as a liar or a fool. (Fool is better. Fools, at least, can be trusted.)

But everyone does something well and everyone wants the assurance that others recognize it. When you offer that assurance, you help the other person find validation and make yourself just a bit more welcome at the next party.

When you give people credit, they start to think they owe you something.

My Story...
- _____
- _____

It's a 10-16, Run for the Hills

What kind of calls do cops really, really, really hate? It's a 10-16, a domestic disturbance. Two proud members of the constabulary arrive at some house, find the master of the domain wailing on his wife and wrestle him to the ground. As soon as the cuffs are on, though, the lady of the estate comes after the cops like a mountain lion on PCP. Claws out, she's defending her mate.

And what do we learn from this? Cops have training, partners, hundreds of other cops to call for backup, cuffs, batons and, oh yes, guns. And they hate getting in the middle of a domestic disturbance.

Be warned. Be careful. Be very, very afraid. Getting in the middle of someone else's fight is like begging for enemies.

When Sally says her boyfriend is cheap, let it go. Don't nod, don't agree, don't smile, don't blink. When Sally is done ragging about her beau, she won't think he's cheap anymore. He's frugal and concerned about saving for the future—his future with Sally. But you! *You* think he's cheap. *You* don't understand how special he is, how special their love is. *You* are just jealous.

When Allan and Rich ask you to settle an argument about who has a better sense of humor, who has better business sense, who is smarter or whose children are prettier, curl up into a ball and roll into the corner. Like the candidate who gets asked, *"Have you stopped beating your wife?"* any answer is fraught with peril. Allan and Rich will forget about their argument, but each will remember how you took the other's side in the debate.

Cops get paid to get in the middle of someone else's fight. Why would anyone else do it for free?

> It's dangerous to watch a fight from inside the ring.

My Story...

- _____
- _____
- _____
- _____

Oh, Well, God Must Have Hated the Rest of Them

Whenever there's a tragic accident that leads to loss of life, you can count on the local newspaper to quote some survivor who says, *"It just wasn't my time. God was looking out for me and saved me from certain death."*

What the heck does that say about the people who died? *"I guess God has cataracts and couldn't see them?"* *"God never liked them anyway?"* *"God thinks people who sit in rows 22-31 are evil?"*

Imagine the scene in 1865, after John Wilkes Booth and other assassins launch their attack on Union leadership. Imagine the witness who says, *"God was looking out for Ed Stanton, but he really didn't like Honest Abe."*

In any tragedy, there is always someone who rushed to make the flight and someone who got caught in a lifesaving traffic jam, someone who turned to the left and someone who walked through the wrong door. In hindsight, we know which was which, but that doesn't help us figure out what's coming next.

But maybe you're different. Maybe you're smarter, faster, more intuitive and you decide you can prevent disaster. You lock the car doors so nobody can carjack you and you adjust the mirrors and position your seat and you're driving just under the limit and checking your blind spots when, wham, some guy on a cell phone rear-ends you. And then something hits you, besides the guy on the cell phone. Suddenly, you realize that you can take all kinds of precautions, but you really don't control very much.

There's a story that made the rounds in Chicago a number of years ago about a tragedy at a construction site. I'm not really sure this story is true, but it's such a good example that we will assume, for the sake of our discussion, that it is 100 percent accurate.

The construction crew was building a parking ramp and a workman with a wheelbarrow was hauling some junk. Then he slipped. The wheelbarrow started rolling forward and he kept trying to stop it.

The wheelbarrow gathered speed and, in a few seconds, both he and the wheelbarrow went over the edge of the building and he fell to his death.

My Story...

- _____
- _____
- _____
- _____

Now, all this man had to do to save his life was let go. But he didn't. He held on to the handles of the wheelbarrow, trying to control its motion. And while he focused on that one thing, he gave up everything else.

We're a lot like that (possibly imaginary) guy. We keep a firm grasp on a few things and confuse our death-grip with control. It's not, of course. Life has too many moving parts, and we can only influence a handful of them over the long term.

Control is an illusion.

Life's Greatest Gift

The greatest gift you can give anyone isn't a Rolex or a Rolls Royce or even Roller Blades. The greatest gift cannot be bought, sold, bartered, manufactured, stored, saved or replaced.

The greatest gift is time.

Time is infinite, but our time is not. When we give someone our time, we are giving something truly priceless and unique. None of us knows how much time we have in this world, but we can be absolutely sure that, at this time tomorrow, we'll have 24 fewer hours to live.

Our most cherished memories are of time: prom night, passing the driving test, taking a trip with the family, Thanksgiving dinner at Aunt Edna's, the day we cut class with our friends to go to Opening Day.

Yes, there are a few physical gifts that we continue to treasure throughout our lives. Usually, though, these gifts are connected to an event, to a rite of passage. The day we bought our first car was a big deal, but most of us realize it wasn't the car itself that was truly important. The big deal was what the car represented to us.

It was the fact we had reached maturity, gained independence, achieved the financial capacity to afford a new car that was significant.

Ask a thoughtful person what he wishes he had, and the answer will probably involve time. Time to read, time to spend with friends or children, time to learn a new language or travel the world. Ask about a person's regrets and the answer will often begin, *"I wish I could go back in time and..."* or *"I wish I had spent more time with...."*

Time is a gift that can only be given once and can never be experienced in the same way again. In fact, time cannot be experienced the same way by two people. No matter how you give it, time can never be returned or exchanged. That makes it unique—and priceless.

Sharing time is the gift of a life.

My Story...

- _____
- _____
- _____
- _____

I Knew What I Was Doing All The Time

Many years ago, probably before you were born or maybe even before there were personal computers and cell phones, there was a guy who decided to fly in a lawn chair. Really. He tied a bunch of helium balloons to a lawn chair, cut the tether and soared into the nearest flight path.

Oddly, he lived. He didn't get hit by any planes—although he did come a bit too close to one—and he didn't fall off his chair. After awhile aloft, he burst a few balloons to get back down and ended up on lots of talk shows. And he explained that he wasn't in any danger because he knew what he was doing all along.

Which brings us to our lesson for today: just because something goes right, that doesn't make it smart. When I was younger, I drove several times after having too much to drink. I didn't kill anyone, including myself, but that doesn't make me capable. It makes me lucky, maybe luckier than I deserve. Also, it makes me stupid.

Conversely, we can be very smart and still miss the mark. We can study the stock market, consult with experts, make seemingly safe investments, and still lose our shirts. We can plan the perfect party, attend to every detail, and end up with a boring evening.

When we fail, we sometimes kick ourselves for bad decisions. But just because something doesn't work out doesn't mean the idea itself was bad. Sometimes, great ideas don't turn into great results, and sometimes people succeed in spite of the stupid things they do.

We have a knack for ascribing great wisdom to people who succeed, as if their success was somehow preordained. In most cases, though, we can find ten or twenty or a hundred other people who tried the same things, had the same ideas, maybe did a better job by some objective standard—but failed anyway.

Ascribing wisdom in hindsight is like driving by looking in your rearview mirror. Even if you don't get in an accident, it's still dumb.

Good practice is good practice. Making good decisions leads to success more often than making stupid decisions. Yeah, somebody is going to split fours and hit 21 twice. Most likely, though, that person won't be you.

Don't do stupid things.

My Story...
- _____
- _____

Nobody Gets Out of High School

Not many people get through high school without big, throbbing scars across their psyches. High school is a tough town, where kids going through the upheaval of puberty must also confront the new social strata that were only beginning to form in seventh and eighth grades. Two thousand kids with raging hormones and a lost sense of identity converge to read *Lord of the Flies*—and then bring the book to life.

Almost all of us have some high school trauma that comes to mind every so often, an embarrassment that makes us cringe even when we're fifty years old.

You can be living in a new town, out of touch with everyone you knew when you were young, in relationships with people who have no idea where you came from or what you were like in your teens. And then...something comes up in conversation and you panic, because you know that all your new friends remember when everyone called you *Zitface*.

The pain grows less intense as the years pass, but the twinges never disappear completely. Then, one day, we recognize the great gift given to us during our four, five or six years in high school. Finally, we see the upside of our suffering.

Suddenly, one day, we realize that high school trauma is the great equalizer. Rich or poor, smart or dumb, fancy or plain, no matter who we were or who we became, we're all the same. All of us, even the most famous and successful among us, remember ourselves as the gawky, insecure, clumsy losers of our teenage years.

And how does that help us? Because it puts us on the same plane as everyone else. The meeting with the potential employer? She hasn't gotten over the fact that she went to prom with her cousin, Judy. The doctor? He still cringes when he remembers having to take a shower after gym.

"Wait," you say again. *"What about the jocks and the cheerleaders, the people who ruled the hallways and lived like royalty in high school? I'll bet they only wish they were still in school."*

Ah, yes, the chosen few. Truth be told, many of them weren't all that happy in high school. Just as we think the rich and famous are somehow happier than we

My Story...
- _____
- _____
- _____
- _____

are, we often overestimate the joys of high school for the *in crowd.*

Meanwhile, the people who really, truly think high school was the best time of their lives are trapped worse than the rest of us. What does it mean to be thirty, forty, fifty years old and still, to this day, think you peaked at eighteen? Purgatory on earth.

No doubt, there are a handful of well-adjusted people who remember a great high-school experience and lived to become productive, decent adults. It's a safe bet, though, that the next person you meet, no matter how big and important and smart and tough, won't be one of those happy few. Us. Them. Same difference.

> High school is the cure for wishing we were young again.

Percolation

Does anyone make coffee in percolators any more? Or is everyone using drip machines? Whatever. The concept is the same.

Percolation is the passage of a liquid through solids, like coffee grounds or rock formations, dissolving some of the solids as it travels. Percolation is how hot water becomes coffee and it's how thoughts become beliefs.

Percolation is a good technique when you're making big decisions. Study the issue, then let it sit for a day or two. Your brain will be sorting things out without much conscious thought. When you get back to the topic, new perspective and insight will often appear, simply because you took the time to let the issue percolate.

I discovered percolation years ago, when I actually tried to take calculus in college. I was failing through most of the semester and I needed to ace the final in order to pass the course.

The night before the final, I sat down with the book and (Don't let your kids see this.) a six-pack of beer. I read everything I could and finished the book and the beer at the same time. I still didn't get it, so I gave up and went to sleep.

The next day, I aced the final. Yes, I could probably get a much better endorsement deal if I said the beer improved my memory, but the truth is that my brain connected the dots while I was sleeping. When I wasn't even thinking about it, or possibly *because* I wasn't thinking about it, my brain did whatever brains do to make sense of the world.

Percolation. Your brain organizes all kinds of stuff, if you let it. So when somebody tells you, *"Why don't you sleep on it? Things will look clearer in the morning,"* take their advice.

This is a particularly useful technique when your best friend, worst enemy or most annoying customer sends you an e-mail that really ticks you off big-time. Sure, you have to respond, but after you write your response, don't hit send. Let it percolate overnight and then re-read it. The benefits are huge.

The answer will come to the surface, if we have the smarts to wait.

My Story...

- _____
- _____
- _____
- _____

How's Your Gut?

Remember Cassandra, the Greek oracle? Of course you don't. You slept through that class, or you didn't bother to take notes. Like, who is ever going to ask you about Cassandra, anyway?

Okay, so Cassandra was a Greek oracle with a really creative curse: her prophecies would always come true, but none of them would be believed. Today, when someone (much older than you) calls a person a Cassandra, they mean that person is a false prophet of doom. Unfortunately, they miss the irony of the story.

So why are we wandering through Greek mythology? Because all of us are prophets of greater or lesser skill, and misjudge our own ability to anticipate the future. All kinds of people will tell you to go with your gut. Trust your instincts. You'll know it when you see it.

And that might be true...or not. I know a person whose instincts are almost 100 percent, absolutely, predictably, guaranteed to be wrong. This person is a great bellwether and sounding board, but not for the reason that this person thinks. (Notice that I'm not even noting the person's gender because I am guaranteed to get questions on this from just about everyone I've ever asked for advice.)

This person is an extreme case, but all of us have varying degrees of predictive and intuitive skills, depending on the topic or circumstances or our state of mind. So it's important to figure out how all this *trust-your-gut* stuff works for you. When you go with your gut, when you make a snap decision, are you usually successful or do you make matters worse? Does it depend on the subject or risk level? Some people are better with short-term decisions than long, or better with finance than emotion. Or vice versa.

Which are you? When you decide to trust your gut, should you trust it to be right or assume that it's wrong? If MapQuest always gave you the wrong directions, you'd stop relying on it. Why should you treat your instincts any differently?

Right or wrong, our instincts will predict the way to go.

My Story...

- _____
- _____
- _____
- _____

We All Have 20/5 Vision

From a distance, everything is absolutely clear. You and I, we could fix pretty much every problem for every person anywhere in the world. We know what our friends should do if they want to solve their problems. We know even better what the president should do, what the Pope should do and, absolutely, which people should be voted off the island.

In fact, unlike real vision, our clarity gets better with greater distance. The more detached we are from a situation, the clearer the paths appear. I'm not mocking this perception. In some ways, we really do see things more clearly from a distance.

From a distance, we see the big picture. We can ignore the small stuff that gets in the way of good decisions and we can dismiss the minor *buts* and *what ifs* that really aren't germane to the topic anyway.

So why don't other people pay attention when we offer our big-picture insights? Because, as noted earlier, people tend to want validation more than they want help. Even when they ask for advice, their defenses kick in as soon as we offer it.

Admit it. You do the same. You ask somebody for advice and you might really want to know the good and the bad. But as soon as the comments turn critical, the walls go up and you begin to think of reasons why none of this applies to you.

I love you like you're my child, but you know it's true. When someone tells you what you should do, the shields go up and you're at Defcon One. You cross your arms and sit back in your chair and look like you're about to pull a blanket over your head.

Now, I've already told you that nobody but you can solve your problems and I know how defensive you get when people criticize you, so I won't make any suggestions about what you should do. Instead, I'll tell you about a technique I use when I'm the one with the issue.

I adopt two roles and argue with myself. After all, who knows better the barriers I'll erect and the arguments I'll raise? I'm a really tenacious adversary and the battle can rage for days, off and on: insight, defense, acknowledgement, rephrasing, admission, repositioning,

My Story...

- _____
- _____
- _____
- _____

acceptance, point, counterpoint, thesis, antithesis, synthesis.

Ultimately, though, I tire myself out and accept the truth, even if it's a painful admission and one I've been fighting for years. And here's the best part: Once the battle is over, I'm more at peace with myself.

> Talking to yourself can be very, very smart.

They Have Ten, You Have Zip

My mom used to keep track of what people gave me for birthdays and other special occasions, so she would know how much to spend on gifts for their kids. I thought this was a bit (a bit?) excessive, but then I found out lots of moms do this.

Keeping track of gifts is just one of the ways we keep score in life. We all do it in one way or another. How much money am I making compared to the other people in my class? How many promotions did I get versus the guy who started the same week I did? How many pounds have my friends gained since graduation compared to me?

We keep score to assess our progress in life and we do it by comparing ourselves to friends, family, neighbors, colleagues, pretty much everyone we know. Have I advanced enough in my career? What's enough? Well, Betty started the same time I did. How am I doing compared to her?

Keeping score has its value, but it shouldn't be a zero-sum game. Somebody else's success doesn't make you worse off, and your success doesn't really harm somebody else.

We can always find people doing better in any given area—and at least an equal number doing worse. Plus or minus 300 million people, we're pretty much in the middle of the pack. What really happens, though, is that we use score-keeping for self-flagellation. We slant the score by comparing ourselves with those who are doing better, ignoring those who are less fortunate.

It's only natural. Why would I compare myself with Ed? He barely got through school and jumped right into a bottle of bourbon. Gail? Please! She has no work ethic and she couldn't make it at her dad's clothing store.

When we keep score, we compare ourselves with the wunderkinder, and we always lose. We pretty much shift the scales so that our position is all the way at the bottom and everyone else is at the top.

If somebody else was abusing us this badly, we'd call the cops. When we do it to ourselves, we think we're insightful.

If you're going to fix a fight, fix it so you win.

My Story...
- _____
- _____

You'd Do It, Too

I was sitting in a bar with a cop I used to know, talking about a brawl involving the young adult offspring of some very well-connected individuals. People were hurt, severely, in the incident and you could almost hear the hum of strings being pulled and debts being called in as the parents scrambled to get their kids out of jail and leave all the talking to their lawyers.

So I said how disgusted I was by the race to protect people from the consequences of their actions and how it must be frustrating for cops to deal with the political meddling.

He stared at me for a few seconds. *"You'd do it, too,"* he said.

I didn't have children yet, so he enlightened me. It doesn't matter whether your kids are guilty or innocent and it doesn't matter what the facts are. Parents protect their children first and ask questions later. Even when they don't believe what their kids tell them, they make the decision to believe *in them*. Even when the situation is a public disturbance or scandal, it's a family issue first.

The lesson applies to much more than children, though. Very often, we're critical of others for actions that we would copy if we were in their shoes, whether it's a parent trying to block a well-deserved suspension from high school or a Wall Streeter accepting an unearned bonus, a rock star dodging child support or a politician accepting courtside seats from a *friend*.

Indignation and fulmination consume tons of energy, most of which is wasted when we direct it at people we don't know and never expect to meet. When we realize our target has committed an offense that we'd emulate, if only we could, our response is not just a waste of energy, it's hypocritical, as well.

> More often than we care to admit, the difference between us and them is access, not ethics.

My Story...
- _____
- _____
- _____
- _____

You Can't Always Get What You Want

So I was sitting around one day, thinking about some things that I would like to have and some other things I'd like to do and how much money I didn't have to pay for all of those things, and I was getting just a bit depressed about the whole thing.

I'd been working a lot of years and I was doing well by all global standards. I wasn't doing as well as the people I was benchmarking against, of course, but that's the way it is when you keep score. Still, I was doing better than I'd ever thought I might when I was growing up in Chicago.

Didn't matter. I didn't have it and I wasn't going to get it. No matter how well off I was. I was never going to afford the stuff I really wanted. Some of this was stuff I had never heard of when I was growing up. Most of the hi-tech stuff didn't even exist when I was a kid and some belonged to the world of *haves*, where my family didn't even have a one-day guest pass.

It was all a bit overwhelming and, even in my frenzy of avarice, I recognized that I was overly obsessed with *things*. Why did I care so much about possessions that wouldn't make me happy anyway?

And then I had an epiphany, when reality and common sense burst through my fortress of envy.

I'd made a choice. I'd chosen to consider my personal achievement in terms of *things*. Worse, I had chosen to place more value on the things I wanted than on the things I already had. I wanted things until I had them, but once I'd had them, I didn't care about them any more. I wanted the next thing. Why? Because I didn't have it yet.

Millions of us think this way, and pretty much every one of us is foolish. If it's worth getting, it's worth having, but sometimes we devalue our goals once we've achieved them. It's like our possessions are a one-night stand.

Suddenly, a life-changing question came to mind. What if I decide to want what I already have? What if I decide to value my possessions after I've obtained them? What if I invested all that longing and desire to obtain an actual payoff?

My Story...

- _____
- _____
- _____
- _____

I hadn't really thought about it, but wanting what I don't have was something I learned. Maybe it was advertising and maybe it was dinner table conversation about the families that had moved into houses instead of apartments. Whatever the case, wanting what I didn't have wasn't genetic. It was learned.

So I taught myself to want what I already have, to appreciate the comfort of my own bed and the features of my own car and the reliability of my old camera. Once I decided to do it, the entire change of attitude took about a week. Awareness can do that for you.

Sure, there are still things I want, things I'll work to get. But they don't have the same pull as before. I don't find myself lacking, because I decided to like what I already have. And when I get the next things I want, I'll keep on liking them, too.

> If I want what I have, I have what I want.

The Burning Bush

There was this gawd-awful-ugly plant by the front door of our first house. Why someone would put it by the entry was beyond me. This bush had big, shapeless leaves, growing in all directions, with no symmetry or proportion.

Whenever I walked past it, I was tempted to grab a shovel and dig it out, down to its grotesque roots.

And then came autumn. As the chlorophyll receded, the leaves on this bush turned an intense, ruby red. The eruption of color was breathtaking, all the more so because the plant had been so unattractive until then. I stared at the bush each time I came into the house, mesmerized both by its beauty and its transformation.

People are like that bush. Sometimes, there's a person who seems to have no place in the world, nothing to add, no particular talent or opportunity to make the world a better place. We ignore them; some of us mock them. If they have anything to add at all, it certainly isn't obvious. Sometimes, in our pasts, we have been that person.

Then, one day...

Be nice to everyone you meet: busboys, cab drivers, waitresses, garbage men, beggars, maids, fast-food servers—everyone. They might not be the person who's going to pull you from a burning car. But you don't really know that, do you?

Everybody has a gift, even if it's not obvious at first glance.

My Story...
- _____
- _____
- _____
- _____

Because I Like the Pain So Much

I love bad surprises. I don't mean that I love for bad things to happen. It's just that, if something bad is going to happen, I'd prefer to be surprised. Otherwise, I end up suffering twice—once while anticipating the problem and again when it actually occurs.

Lots of people I know—not you, of course—worry about all sorts of things they can't control. There's an endless array of serious and silly topics to worry about and we all have something in our repertoire. *"What if they don't like me? What if they don't think I'm worthy? What if I get toenail cancer? What if I trip down the stairs and drop my I-Phone?"*

The list is potentially endless, and some of us seem to have an endless list prepared. Before anything bad happens, we force ourselves to anticipate and experience the pain of rejection, embarrassment or loss. Sometimes, we stress about a situation so much, we experience more pain than the situation could possibly create.

So who volunteers for this kind of abuse? Well, all of us at one point or another. But we could give ourselves a break, and we would, if we didn't like the pain so much.

> Trouble follows its own schedule; don't make special plans to meet it.

My Story...
- _____
- _____
- _____
- _____

This Chapter Will Exceed Your Expectations

On Wall Street, nobody cares how much money a company makes. What they really care about is how much a company makes in comparison with what they already expected. A company can triple its earnings, but if people were expecting something even a penny better, the stock will go down.

We're a lot like the stock market. We don't always accept things as they are, but judge them in comparison to expectations. And when we build up our expectations, we almost always end up disappointed.

My wife and I went to a restaurant in Atlanta run by two women who had some cooking skills and time on their hands. It was one of the best meals we ever had. The food was great, the atmosphere was warm, and we couldn't wait to tell our friends.

So we told some friends about this phenomenal find, about the meal they simply couldn't miss, and they made sure to visit the next time they were in Atlanta. Then they came back and told us it was one of the worst dining experiences they'd ever had.

We were on the receiving end of a best-restaurant recommendation a few years later. We were heading to

New York for our anniversary weekend and a partner told me about the most fabulous, romantic, dining experience in all of New York City. Of course, it came nowhere close to matching the hype.

Hype, of course, is short for hyperbole, which is another way of saying *impossible*. Nothing measures up to its hype. The more we promise, the more we ensure that the result will be underwhelming. Perhaps our experiences, and those of our friends, would have been less disappointing if we hadn't set the bar so high.

The same thing applies to our dealings with other people. When we have high expectations for them, they usually try to rise to the challenge. When we demand perfection, however, they often decide not to bother with the exercise at all. If they cannot help but disappoint, why expend the energy? They know they can't live up to the hype. The same applies when we set impossible standards for ourselves.

Satisfaction comes from expectations that are met and promises that are kept.

My Story...
- _____
- _____

Fighting Words

So you've read all the bits of wisdom in this book and your life isn't perfect yet? Obviously, the problem is that *you* aren't paying attention. Everyone else was deliriously happy by the time they were done with chapter three. Why don't *you* try harder?

So how do you feel when you read a paragraph like the one above? Most likely, a bit angry, offended, insulted, attacked. Even if everything I said is true—and it couldn't possibly be for an exceptionally wise reader like you—you'd still be irritated, because I used *fighting words*.

Fighting words are accusations disguised as statements of fact or, worse, helpful advice. How do you recognize a sentence with fighting words? The subject of the sentence is almost always one word: *you*.

You didn't send me the e-mail. *You* should watch where you're going. *You* don't understand anything about me. *You* should have called me sooner/later/yesterday/never.

When we start a sentence with *you*, we draw a line between ourselves and the other person. Often, we use this device defensively, to deflect blame or absolve ourselves of responsibility. We all do it, but it ticks people off and it doesn't add much to the quality of life.

"You didn't send me the e-mail," is an accusation. *"I didn't get the e-mail,"* is less so. *"I don't remember getting the e-mail, but it might still be in my inbox,"* is fairly neutral.

Almost always, "we" is better than "you." *"We"* puts us in the same boat, sharing the same problems and solutions. *"You"* places a wall between us.

> YOU should stop using fighting words.

My Story...

- _____
- _____
- _____
- _____

Always Stop for a Bier

Back when I worked as a newspaper reporter, I knew a guy in public office. Not particularly interesting or charismatic, to my mind, but he was very popular on Election Day. What was behind his immense appeal to voters? He had been a local funeral director for many, many years.

Nobody really cared that much about his positions or his personality, but they all remembered how nice and comforting he was when Aunt Clara or Uncle Frank or Cousin Sophie died. Despite all the jokes and stereotypes, most people like and respect funeral directors because they help us get through some very difficult times.

We can't all become funeral directors, no matter how much we wish for the privilege, but we can earn the same reputation as top morticians around the globe. All we have to do is show up at funerals. Sure, it's a bit uncomfortable, but it's a good deed that nobody forgets.

That's because funerals are only partly about the deceased and mostly about the mourners. Mourners need to know someone cared about their loved ones, but they need equally to know someone cares about them. Even if you're not interested in public office, funeral attendance is a lot more important—and appreciated—than most people think.

The same rule applies whenever somebody is going through tough times. When I got fired from my job (company president, 300 employees, tons of vendors), I was stunned at the number of people who lost my phone number. Worse, they even forgot my name, so they didn't return my calls.

After talking to others who experienced similar setbacks, I found I wasn't alone. At the exact time they needed others the most, they found out how shallow and false many friendships were. After experiencing this disappointment, I've been more attentive to others who suffer a loss.

It's amazing how much they appreciate this kindness. And it's sad to know how rare it is.

When we're all alone in the world, we meet our real friends.

My Story...
- _____
- _____

Another Meeting with the PTA

When a person is considered for sainthood in the Catholic Church, the review process is much like a trial, with representatives who speak both for and against the individual. The person assigned to defame and disqualify the candidate is known as *the devil's advocate.*

Unfortunately, the devil's advocate is alive and well in all of our lives and scores number one on my personal PTA (People To Avoid) list. You know the type I mean. No matter what your idea, no matter how lofty the goal, the devil's advocate will offer a hundred reasons why it won't work and no suggestions for making it better.

"Let me play devil's advocate for a moment," our friend will say, following up with an endless list of traps, landmines and seeds of failure.

"Don't throw that life preserver to that drowning man," the devil's advocate will warn us. *"What if it hits him and knocks him unconscious and he drowns and his family sues you? What if the line gets caught in the propeller and pulls him under? What if...oh, too late. Never mind."*

What's with these people? Deep inside, they want to avoid accountability at all costs. They delay and derail initiatives and make progress more difficult. They don't care about obtaining credit for success as much as they desperately seek to avoid blame for any failure. By issuing as many warnings and caveats as possible, they seek a guarantee that they can say, *"I told you so."*

Every issue has its supporters and detractors, and healthy debate is good for all of us. But the devil's advocate takes the negative position 99 percent of the time and ducks responsibility for answering his own questions. If you run into one of these people, keep running. If you are one, stop it.

> The devil's advocate is never on the side of the angels.

My Story...
- _____
- _____
- _____
- _____

Somebody Else's Secret

I know way too much stuff that's none of my business, which is another way you and I are sooooooo much alike. For my part, I keep a virtual file cabinet in the back of my head, sort of a recycle bin for data I want to trash. Whenever possible, I delete the memories of things I shouldn't know and I'm much happier for it.

We end up knowing more than we should about who's sleeping with whom, whose car got repossessed, who flunked out of kindergarten and who picks his nose at stoplights. Some of this stuff we know because it's in the newspaper and on the internet every day, mostly about people we'll never meet and probably wouldn't like anyway.

The stuff that's more discomfiting is the information we get about people we know. Sometimes, they offer their secrets because someone said it was good to share, to let it all out. Sometimes the source of too much information is an overheard cell phone conversation or an e-mail sent to *Reply All*. In the worst cases, a best friend betrays a confidence in the misguided belief that other people *have a right to know*.

There are many kinds of secrets, of course. Some are minor and nobody really cares if they become known.

More dangerous are the secrets that would cause embarrassment or harm reputations. If it's the latter, beware. Once the owner shares the secret with someone else, all control is lost.

As Ben Franklin noted, the only way for three people to keep a secret is if two of them are dead. Smart guy, Ben was.

Trauma. Betrayal. Alienation. Retribution. All of these are the predictable and wholly avoidable results of sharing someone else's secret. And, as noted a number of pages back, the secret cannot be untold after it's revealed.

> *Secrets are property. Don't give away something you don't own.*

```
My Story...
  •  _____
  •  _____
  •  _____
  •  _____
```

Mahatma and Me

One day you'll be in a room full of people and someone will mention a good deed. It could be a charitable donation or a mentoring program or some historical lesson from the great sages of history.

Let's say, for example, that someone points out the selfless dedication of Mother Teresa in tending to the poor and sick of Calcutta. Almost immediately, someone will jump in to detail her own generosity to others. Almost invariably, the first person to speak about her own generosity will turn out to be the person least like Mother Teresa.

I'm sure there's a deep psychological explanation for this, but I never earned a psych degree, so here's my untutored explanation. The people in the room who are really generous will recognize how much their efforts pale in comparison to the life work of Mother Teresa—so they shut up. The least generous person won't recognize the size of the void, so he'll assert some equivalence between letting the staff go home an hour early and caring for lepers.

Like our devil's advocate, these are People to Avoid. They have stingy souls and lack self-awareness. They'll overstate the importance of anything they do for you and expect you to repay any favor ten times over. This is a very broad statement, but that doesn't make it false.

People with halos don't need a spotlight.

My Story...
- _____
- _____
- _____
- _____

I'm Sorry I Didn't Mention This Sooner

There is a two-word phrase that has the power to save relationships, avoid violence, win friends and bring a smile to the faces of millions. Totaling a mere seven letters, this phrase comprises the most powerful words in the English language.

"I'm sorry."

This phrase is so powerful that adding more words detracts from its power. *"I'm sorry,"* is so much better than *"I'm sorry, but...."* or *"I'm sorry that you didn't...."* or *"I'm sorry they...."* Most of the time, the more you add, the more you take away.

It's possible to add insight to an apology, but there's a fine line between adding information and making an excuse. It's one thing to say we tried and failed and quite another to say someone or something else was to blame.

I know a person who is fond of saying, *"I'm sorry I was late, but I left early enough to get here on time."* This *"apology"* is unsatisfying for two reasons.

First, it absolutely cannot be true. If the person left early enough to arrive on time, he wouldn't be late. Second, the excuse makes it sound like the person isn't sorry at all, but is just going through the motions. Think back to all the unconvincing apologies you've received—or given. Most likely, they included an explanation that was really an excuse that nullified two simple and powerful words.

"I'm sorry."

Learn how to say it. Learn how to say it like you mean it. Practice it so much that you really do mean it when you say it. You will become more successful in life and more at peace with all people—including yourself.

> It's easiest to accept an apology when it's not excepted.

My Story...
- _____
- _____
- _____
- _____

> One Hundred Percents

Cause and effect. What a simple concept. And what a flawed idea it is.

Causes and effects is much more accurate, because there is almost never just one cause or just one effect. Too frequently, somebody or something gets way too much credit, or blame, because we decide to boil it all down to one cause and one effect.

When I was about twelve, I read a story about a plane that crashed on takeoff. The story focused on all the little things that added up to doom the flight. As I recall the tale, the runway was shortened by some repair work at one end, the trees just beyond the runway had grown, the pilot underestimated the takeoff distance because he subtracted the weight of fuel instead of adding it...and the plane was doomed to hit the trees as it took off.

In life, what occurs is the combination of hundreds of variables. Some are controllable and others not, some predictable and others random. The search for a single cause is distracting and misleading. Often, it leads us to place credit or blame where it doesn't belong and it encourages us to repeat bad behaviors.

In the worst of cases, we get it absolutely backwards. Sometimes, people conclude something happened as a result of some factor, when in reality it happened in spite of that factor. Focus on the wrong coincidence and you begin to follow a path of failure, rather than a route to success.

> Nothing is one hundred percent. Everything is one hundred percents.

My Story...
- _____
- _____
- _____
- _____

One Thing at a Time

I used to worry about all the things I had to do and I was always overwhelmed with the workload that faced me. But my dad explained to me that I could handle all of it, if only I faced one thing at a time.

Multitasking is a myth. We like to think we're phoning and e-mailing and sipping energy drinks and doing our filing at the same time, but we're kidding ourselves. In reality, we just do everything less well in more time. Why? When we mentally shift gears, our brains need time to close out one process and begin to connect to another. It's just like closing one program and opening another on a computer, except we don't see any cool icons spinning in front of us.

With even the simplest task, some time is lost as we shift gears and refocus. Divide three hours of work into 50 multitasked segments and the total effort will expand to four hours—and it won't be done as well. Thoughtful effort requires preparation and focus, which improve with undivided attention. Break the focus and break the spell. All the magic disappears.

People get distracted by trying to drive while on their cell phones, eating a breakfast sandwich and checking the headlines in the morning paper. None of these tasks is particularly complicated, of course. Combined, they can be fatal.

Maybe I can do it all, but I can't do it all at once.

My Story...
- _____
- _____
- _____
- _____

It all Happens at the Margin

You're overscheduled. You can't keep up. You hardly have time to read your e-mails and you've started dining in your car on the way home from work to save a few minutes. There are 24 hours in a day, so why isn't there time for anything?

Because there aren't 24 hours in a day. There are only five or six. And if you're working overtime to get ahead in the world, there might be only two or three. Welcome to life, where everything happens at the margin.

Let's assume that you're working for a living, you commute an average distance and you eat two meals per day. So here's how a day breaks down:

Hours Activity

- 8   Work. (Actually, many people end up at the office for nine hours or more, due to overtime or structured work days or whatever.)
- 8   Sleep. (Yeah, some people say they can get by on six hours a night, but these people are rare. Lots of people sleep less than eight hours during the week, but then make up for it by sleeping 12 hours on weekends.)

2	Eating. (Whether you cook or eat at a restaurant, you'll spend about two hours a day at the trough.)
1	Ablutions. (This is a quaint term for showering, shaving, applying makeup, etc.)
1	Commuting. (It usually takes an hour to get to and from work. In the big city, it's probably closer to two hours; three if you live in the suburbs.)
2	Everything else that you *have to do*. (Paying bills, talking to mom, shopping for groceries, taking in the dry cleaning, doing the laundry, talking to mom again, walking the dog, cleaning the apartment, getting the oil changed, filling the tank, talking to mom again, buying clothes, getting prescriptions refilled, talking to mom again.)
2	Everything else that you want to do. (Watching television, Twittering, downloading MP3s, updating your Facebook wall, going to grad school, volunteering for charity, seeing friends, exercising, applying for a better job, etc.)

So that's 24 hours. One full day. And in that day, you only have two hours to spend on all the things you actually want to do. No time to spare, unless you give up sleep or move closer to the office or stop showering (not recommended) or stop talking to your friends…and mom.

My Story...
- _____
- _____

Let's assume that you're working to get ahead in the world, so you end up at the office an extra hour. And maybe you spend a bit more time in bed or in the ablution room. So how many hours are there in a day? Maybe zero. Maybe less than zero. So you end up with lots of errands to do on the weekend, and you wonder why there wasn't enough time to get these jobs done during the week.

Maybe you're one of the lucky ones who lives five minutes from the office and gets by on six hours of sleep. You still have only a few hours a day to do everything you want; 80 percent of your day is spoken for before you get up.

The same rule applies to money. Where does it all go? First, there are luxuries like food and rent, then transportation and cleaning supplies and clothes and medicine. Free cash? Maybe that's only 10 percent of the total, or maybe it's zero.

Here's the good news. It's all manageable. Lots of people find a way to work a job and go to grad school and pay the rent and put money in the 401(k) and talk to friends and walk the dog. It just takes some effort and focus, because all these things happen at the margin, where the last 10-20 percent of everything are yours to enjoy.

The margin is where all the difference gets made.

Rich Folks Like You and Me

I'm one of the richest people in the world. Most likely, you are, as well. According to the *World Institute for Development Economics Research*, the average individual on Terra Firma had $2,200 of assets in 2000. Maybe it's $2,500 now, or $2,700, but that's not a tough standard to beat in the Western world. If your net worth is $3,000 or more, you're in the upper half of global wealth.

But let's say you want to be in the upper 1 percent of global wealth—with net worth of more than $500,000. How are you going to get there?

Spend less than you earn.

Yes, it's pure genius! You could spend hundreds, maybe thousands of dollars on investment books and money guides and an MBA in finance and when you were all done—and really, really, really sophisticated financially—you could boil it all down to just five words.

Spend less than you earn.

How does this magical principle work? Glad you asked. First, when we spend less than we earn, we get money to invest. There are lots of ways to invest money—

too many for a glib and slick book like this one—but the concept is the same for all of them. Market meltdowns notwithstanding, the best way to retire rich is to invest for a long-term return and build a nest egg over time.

Second, when we spend less than we earn, we reduce the amount of savings required for financial security. A person who lives on only half his income can save enough to retire in much less time than someone who lives on 90 percent of his income. That's because he's saving more money to begin with, but needs less money to maintain his lifestyle.

What about the person who's spending 110 percent of earnings? Lotsa luck on that, baby.

"But, gee, I'm not earning enough to save any money," you say. Poppycock. It's a choice you're making. Lattes, beer, shoes, the Beemer, savings—all are choices of how to use your income. The young adult who buys a $5 frappalattechino at some fancy coffee shop each morning could have an extra $150,000 at retirement,

My Story...
- _____
- _____
- _____
- _____

simply by switching to a $1.50 cup of coffee and investing the savings at a conservative rate. Skip the coffee altogether and the retirement payoff is closer to $220,000. After taxes.

Choices, choices, choices. One less pair of shoes per year, three fewer beers per week, two less appetizers and one less dessert per month...it all adds up. It doesn't seem to make much difference in the beginning. Over time, it can be worth $millions.

Sounds easy, but how to get started? *(Big Disclaimer: Your situation is specific, so this advice is not for you, specifically. It's a general principle and I make no assurances of results, safety or anything else.)* If your company has a 401(k) plan or some other pre-tax savings plan, join it immediately. Put in more than you think you can afford; you can reduce the percentage later, if absolutely necessary. Consider investing it in something other than your employer's stock, because you could lose both your income and your savings if your employer goes out of business. When you get a raise, add a percentage point or two to the amount that's going to the 401(k) plan. Since you weren't receiving the raise before, you won't really miss it. And watch the money grow over time. If your employer provides any kind of a match to your donations, consider that an immediate return on investment. If you put in a dollar and the employer matches it with 50 cents, that's a 50 percent return on investment. Yowza! *(Reminder: This is not investment advice and it certainly isn't intended specifically for you.)*

But start early, like yesterday. The big secret—okay, it's not a secret, but most people ignore it and act surprised when it's too late—is that you can get rich with a relatively low savings rate. You just have to start early. Save 5 percent of your income for 45 years and you do lots better than anyone who tries to save 45 percent of his income for just five years. Interest and returns compound and the total impact is huge.

> Getting rich is easier than it looks.

The Domino Effect

So we're watching the Chicago Bears play a game and everyone is worried that they're going to lose. Mostly, that's because the Bears are a Chicago team and that's what Chicago teams do.

They break your heart, but then we're back the next season, saying *"This is the year,"* like a bunch of yokels at a carnival booth. Mostly the Cubs, of course, but the other guys have their way with us, as well.

Some guy on the team runs back two kicks for touchdowns in what apparently is a record of some sort. At the end of the game, the Bears win. But the fans aren't happy, and you know why? Because, if not for those two touchdown runs, the Bears would only have won by a point or two.

And everybody was talking about it the next day. Okay, not everybody, but enough people to make you wonder about little things like common sense.

Because if the guy hadn't run back the kickoff for a touchdown, something else would have happened. Maybe the team would have scored on that series, taking more time off the clock when they did it and leaving less time for the other team to score. Maybe the victory margin would have been the same, or higher, and those record breaking runs actually hurt the stats.

So what's the point of this ridiculously long introduction? It's simply that you cannot change just one thing. Everything is connected somewhere to something else that's connected to something else that's connected to something else. You know, like that story you hear about a butterfly flapping its wings over the ocean and somehow creating a hurricane on the other side of the world.

If someone asked you the question, *"Can you only change one thing and not affect anything else?"* you'd wisely respond that it's impossible. But lots of people make themselves miserable with useless musings about what might have been. So here's a heartening thought: What if the one thing we regret actually saved us from something even worse? What if that fender bender on First Avenue kept us from colliding with a train at Fifth?

If we could change just one thing, would we be smart enough to change it for the better?

My Story...
- _____
- _____

Pay the $2

There's an old adage that says, *"When somebody tells you it's not about the money...it's about the money!"* And even though that axiom is often correct, it's wrong often enough to discredit it as a rule of thumb.

Because, much of the time, it's absolutely not about the money. It's about reaching the end of one's patience or the end of one's willingness to give one more inch or make one more concession to some lying, cheating, do-nothing, stupid, lazy, worthless bastard who has pushed us too far.

I was talking to this guy the other day, and he's mad because the woman who cleans up his apartment every other week isn't doing a good job. So he wants her to do a better job and she wants an extra five dollars for the effort, and he's spending about forty minutes explaining the problem.

Forty minutes. That's eight minutes per dollar. Forty minutes of his life that he'll never get back. Me, either, for that matter.

And he is right when he says it's not about the money. The money is just a token, a symbol of how he is being abused, how he has limited power in the balance between himself and the woman who cleans apartments all week.

It's about winning and losing. If she gets the five bucks, he loses. Battle of wills. The first one to blink, to back down, is a wuss—and he is not going to be a wuss.

And it's about aggravation. There are four options here and he's aggravated with three of them. If he keeps her on the job and she keeps doing the same work, he thinks she's taking advantage of him. If he keeps her and pays her the extra money, he thinks she's taking advantage of him. If he fires her, he has to find somebody new, which is a pain and takes time and the next person might not be any better. Only one option is acceptable, and that's for the woman to do more work for the same money.

So forty minutes into the discussion, I say he should pay her the five dollars or fire her, but either way, he should move on. Because life is short and ours are now forty minutes shorter and it's only five bucks and there are

My Story...

- _____
- _____
- _____

more important things to stew over.

Which makes me a wuss, I guess, but a wuss who's at peace with the world in a way that I wasn't, many years ago, when I was worried about the five dollars. There's a saying, *"Pay the $2,"* which referred to paying a traffic ticket instead of burning up more time fighting City Hall. Okay, it's an old adage and it probably should be, *"Pay the $50,"* today, but the point remains the same.

> Sometimes, the best decision is to write the check and move on.

No, He Just Looks Like Me

One of the smartest things anyone ever said to me came out of the blue and changed my life in ways that were painful and liberating at the same time. I was talking with a few of my colleagues about goals. I said I wanted to be the guy who led the crack team of professionals on really tough projects, the guy everyone went to for solutions, the guy that people followed because they just knew I was going to make everything right.

And one of my friends asked me, *"Mike, have you ever been that guy?"*

And at 48 or 49 years old, I realized that I hadn't. Which probably meant that it wasn't going to happen. I wasn't going to be the guy that people followed instinctively. I am, was and probably always will be an acquired taste. I'm one of those people you like a lot, once you know me, but I'm not the person you'd follow over a cliff.

So I'd spent a lot of years—or maybe decades—thinking about my goal to be someone I was never wired to be. Maybe it's how I grew up, or maybe it's how my brain was wired in utero (which makes it my mom's fault) or maybe it's just karma. In the end, it doesn't matter much how it happened.

What does matter is acceptance. What matters is forgiving yourself for not being an idealized version of you that doesn't match your DNA. And working with what you have to make yourself better.

Really, nobody can fool us longer or more painfully than we fool ourselves. It took a very simple question to reveal my own delusion in a way that hurt—because I wanted to be that guy—and also liberated, because it freed me to focus on the real me.

This isn't about *you*, of course. Only *me*. You don't have any delusions about yourself. Nothing about your self-image and goals that's out of sync with reality. I'm not even sure why I brought it up, but thanks for listening.

> *"I am what I am," Popeye said. It turns out he was smarter than we knew.*

My Story...

- _____
- _____
- _____
- _____

Don't Force It

George Santayana said a fanatic is a person who redoubles his effort when he has forgotten his aim. My dad wasn't as wordy. All he said was, *"Don't force it."*

Usually, he'd say it when I was trying to fix something or make something or otherwise demonstrate that I have absolutely no mechanical skills.

If it requires that much force, he'd say, maybe I was doing it wrong. Like tightening a bolt instead of loosening it, or pushing a door in the wrong direction. If something seemed to require too much effort, maybe it was a good idea to take a step back and look at the job again. Maybe there is an easier way.

We have a tendency, you and I, to view obstacles as barriers to be overcome, which is a good thing. We make progress by getting past the roadblocks, and all those successful people who write memoirs will tell you that your success depends on getting through the throngs of naysayers.

And yet...it's sometimes easier to go around a barrier than through it. Sometimes, we do more damage by forcing our way in than backing up and looking for a new approach. Sometimes, we're like the bad joke about tourists who can't speak the local language, so they talk more loudly and slowly to be understood.

If something doesn't work, it's just possible that we're doing it wrong. Maybe it's a good idea to take a step back and reconsider. *"Don't force it,"* turned out to be great advice, and not just for all those mechanical projects that I'm now smart enough to hire out to people who know their stuff. In fact, this could be a great mantra for life.

> Pushing harder in the wrong direction doesn't get us where we want to go.

My Story...

- _____
- _____
- _____
- _____

The Tallest Guy in the Room

So I got a promotion and the company sent me out of state for a leadership development seminar. Three days to get in touch with our *inner leaders*, become more sensitive to employees, all that stuff.

Two of the trainers took great pains to explain how they, as psychologists and leaders, had overcome all their personal issues on the way to becoming motivational gurus. One pointed out that he had felt insecure about being short, but that was no longer a problem.

Then, on the second day of the program, a vent needed to be adjusted or a screen raised—I forget exactly what it was—and Mr. Totally Secure said, *"Let's ask Tom to do it. He's the tallest guy in the room."*

Okay, so I'm a short guy and I knew there were lots of people taller than I in our group. But I had no idea who the tallest was. Why would I care?

And if Mr. Totally Secure was really over his height issues, he wouldn't care, either. But he did care, apparently, and he revealed just how important it was by knowing who the tallest guy was. So despite his claim, he revealed his insecurities by his actions.

We all reveal ourselves in one way or another. Some people claim to be generous, but always explain that the waitress hasn't earned a full tip. Some people argue that they are not concerned with looks, but spend way too much time commenting on the appearance of others. And we all know people who claim to be completely free of prejudice, but then they start drinking and…

In time, our actions and comments unveil our true selves, our real values and our worst fears. They're displayed to our friends and family, our bosses, customers and colleagues, especially when our actions contradict our protestations.

When we claim to be someone we are not, we establish a ruse that's bound to be discovered, sooner rather than later. The truth is buoyant, so it pops to the surface in spite of our efforts to keep things submerged.

We're often the last to recognize the person behind our masks.

My Story...
- _____
- _____
- _____

The Secret to Happiness

Okay, take this chapter with a grain of salt. It might not be *the* secret to happiness. It might be one of many secrets to happiness. And it might not be a secret at all. It could turn out to be a bunch of things we all know but fail to put into practice.

But it worked for me, and I'm not exactly the most likely candidate to be explaining happiness to other people. I was less than happy for most of my life. Glass half empty, anticipating the worst, that kind of guy.

Now, I'm happy. Not giggly, jumping up and down, Richard Simmons happy. But *happy*. I wake up in the morning glad to see the world and grateful for the day. I find myself smiling a lot more than I used to, and in response to seemingly minor things like chirping birds or a short line at the drive-thru.

I still worry, get cranky or aggravated from time to time. Some people might argue that you can't be happy if you still worry about things, but I disagree. The real world is challenging and we're all human, so we all have good days and bad ones and things that make us just a tad shy of joyful.

But happiness, I've found, is not really connected to the objective realities of our wealth, health, family or location. In short, it's not situational. I know some very successful people who will never be happy and some less successful ones who are pretty content. (Maybe success is more about happiness than money?)

So how did it happen for me? Mostly, by shedding the baggage I'd collected over too many years. Once, I was carrying more baggage than a Samsonite store. Then, one day, I'd gotten rid of enough to tip the scales into the happiness range.

Here's what I learned along the way:

1. **Let it go.** Anger and resentment are acids that destroy the vessel that contains them. If I grabbed a hot frying pan and burned my hands, I'd drop it. I learned to do the same with life's little disappointments.
2. **I'm no big deal**. Yeah, yeah, I know. I'm the most wonderful, special, only me that ever was or will be. Sometimes, though, feeling special makes us believe the world owes us something or that people should

My Story...

- _____
- _____
- _____
- _____

treat us better than they do. Oddly, or maybe not, recognizing how small we are is a good way to put all kinds of things in perspective.

3. **Acceptance, without acquiescence.** It's important to do good in the world, to make the place just a bit better for our having been here. Striving, trying, fighting, all are good things to do. But we don't always win and, if we don't win, it doesn't mean we should be demoralized or angry. I know this sounds like a loser credo, but it's not. It's just a recognition that there are a lot of innings in this game, so we need to have the right attitude every time we're up at bat.

4. **I'm seriously lucky.** Where do I start? I have a roof over my head and enough food on the table, which puts me ahead of more than half the world. Beyond that, there are a million things that are going great for me. Are there bad things, disappointments, problems? Sure. Did I mention that I'm human? But I'm not keeping score. I'm lucky and that's the end of it.

Here's the weirdest part of my transition, or maybe the most obvious part. Nothing changed other than me. Nobody was suddenly nicer, my investments weren't

```
My Story...
  • _____
  • _____
  • _____
  • _____
```

suddenly more valuable, my job didn't get any more interesting. Everything happened on the inside, because happiness isn't about what you have or what other people do. It's all about how you look at the world.

One day, I thought the bad stuff was the norm and the good stuff was the exception. And I was unhappy. Later, I began to think of the good stuff as the norm and the bad stuff as the exception. And I was happy.

I know that sounds too simple to be true. But that's pretty much what happened. And I'm very happy that it did.

Life's a very good place, but only if you think it is.

About the Author

Michael Rosenbaum is a dad, a husband, a friend and a very good listener. He's also a very bright guy; so bright, in fact, that he knows he has lots to learn. And he knows he can learn something new from everyone he meets.

A former reporter and editor for newspapers, magazines and wire services, Michael knows everyone has a story worth hearing. So he listens, and he takes notes, as people reveal their special insights into their corner of the world.

Michael is also a very efficient guy who figured out how to save lots of time and energy by learning from the experiences—and errors—of other people. *"Why duplicate the mistakes of other people,"* he asks, *"when I can come up with tons of new mistakes on my own?"*

A business consultant by trade, Michael is the author of three business texts; former president of *Financial Relations Board*, the nation's largest investor relations agency; co-author of *Pitching Penguins*, a theatrical comedy; founder of *Friends of the Forum*, a non-profit focused on Polish/Jewish dialogue; active in a number of non-profits and a member of the *World Presidents' Organization.*

Other books by Michael Rosenbaum include:

- *Board Perspectives: Building Value Through Investor Relations*, CCH, 2004
- *The Governance Game*, Aspatore, 2003
- *Selling Your Story to Wall Street: The Art and Science of Investor Relations*, McGraw-Hill, 1994